D1295483

TODAY'S SUPERSTARS
Sports

Michelle
WIE

by Geoffrey M. Horn

GARETH**STEVENS**
GS
P U B L I S H I N G
A Member of the WRC Media Family of Companies

Please visit our web site at: www.garethstevens.com
For a free color catalog describing Gareth Stevens Publishing's
list of high-quality books and multimedia programs, call
1-800-542-2595 (USA) or 1-800-387-3178 (Canada).
Gareth Stevens Publishing's fax: (414) 332-3567.

Library of Congress Cataloging-in-Publication Data

Horn, Geoffrey M.
    Michelle Wie / by Geoffrey M. Horn.
      p. cm. — (Today's superstars: sports)
    Includes bibliographical references and index.
    ISBN-13: 978-0-8368-6186-0 (lib. bdg.)
    ISBN-10: 0-8368-6186-8 (lib. bdg.)
    1. Wie, Michelle—Juvenile literature.   2. Golfers—United States—
  Biography—Juvenile literature.   3. Women golfers—United States—
  Biography—Juvenile literature.   I. Title.
    GV964.W54H67   2006
    796.352092—dc22   2005028959

Updated and reprinted in 2007.

This edition first published in 2006 by
Gareth Stevens Publishing
A Member of the WRC Media Family of Companies
330 West Olive Street, Suite 100
Milwaukee, WI 53212 USA

This edition copyright © 2006 by Gareth Stevens, Inc.

Editor: Jim Mezzanotte
Art direction and design: Tammy West
Picture research: Diane Laska-Swanke

Photo credits: Cover, pp. 5, 9, 10, 12, 17, 24 © AP/Wide World Photos; p. 6
© Alexanderk/WireImage.com; p. 18 © David Cannon/Getty Images; p. 21
© Jonathan Ferrey/Getty Images; p. 26 © Paul Barker/AFP/Getty Images

Printed in the United States of America

1 2 3 4 5 6 7 8 9 10 09 08 07

CONTENTS

CHAPTER 1

A DRIVE TO WIN

A lot of thirteen-year-old girls spend vacations in Florida. But Michelle Wie didn't travel to Palm Coast in June 2003 to work on her tan. She went to write a bright new page in the history of women's golf.

The golf press was already buzzing about the tall eighth-grader from Hawaii. At four years old, Michelle could hit a golf ball 100 yards (91 meters). At eleven, she won two women's tournaments in Hawaii. At thirteen, she could outhit just about every woman pro golfer — and many men, too. She was the next Tiger Woods, some golf experts said. Others said no — she was better than Tiger was at her age.

What did Michelle think of all the hype? "People expect a lot of me," she said. "But I'm not really listening to that. I expect a lot more out of myself than they could."

A Beginner's Guide to Golf

A full-size golf course has eighteen holes, laid out over a wide area. The goal of the game is to sink the ball in each hole, using the fewest possible shots, or strokes.

Courses have both hilly and level parts. They have obstacles such as trees, bushes, rough grass, sand traps, and water hazards. A green is at the end of each hole. It is a mostly level area of smooth, short grass that surrounds the cup and flagstick.

Golfers use different clubs for the many kinds of shots they need to make. They use a driver for the first shot, called the tee shot, or drive. With this shot, the ball travels far, but not usually to the green. Players use other clubs to get the ball to the green, and they use a putter on the green.

Par is the number of strokes a player should need to complete a hole or entire course. Players make a birdie if the number of strokes on a hole is one less than par. They make a bogey if it is one more than par. A double-bogey is two strokes over par.

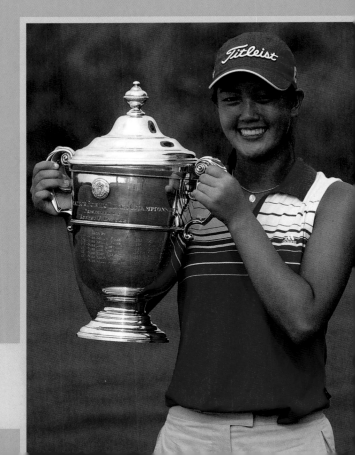

Michelle was only thirteen years old when she won the Publinx tournament in Florida in 2003.

Links to the Title

Michelle had come to Palm Coast to play in the U.S. Women's Amateur Public Links Championship, or Publinx for short. Women of all ages compete for the Publinx crown, and teenagers had won before. In 2000, Catherine Cartwright won the Publinx at the age of seventeen. But until Michelle, no one had expected a thirteen-year-old to have such a serious shot at winning the title.

Now it was time for Wie to show she could live up to the hype — and stand up to the pressure. The competition started

Wie greets reporters after the 2005 Evian Masters in France. Her final-round 68 earned her a tie for second place behind Paula Creamer.

on Tuesday, June 17. Wie didn't wait long to let people know she meant business. A 310-yard (283-m) drive on her very first hole set her up for an easy birdie. She also birdied two of the next four holes, leaving her three under par. But then she lost her lead with a couple of double-bogeys. She finished the first day with a total of 73, one over par for the eighteen-hole course. It wasn't bad, but it was far from her best.

Michelle got off to another fast start on the second day. After the first nine holes, she had two birdies and no bogeys. She completed the round with a score of 71. It was good enough to place her among the top finishers for the first thirty-six holes.

Unstoppable

At the Publinx, the top sixty-four finishers after the first thirty-six holes make it into the playoff rounds. They play matches

FACT FILE

Michelle's last name sounds like WEE. She stands more than 6 feet (1.8 m) tall. Her golf swing looks so smooth that pro golfer Tom Lehman nicknamed her "The Big Wiesy."

against each other, until only one player is left. In these playoffs, nothing could stop Michelle — not even a bloody nose.

While playing a match against Mayumi Motoyama on Friday, her nose began to bleed. But she turned down the offer of medical help. "I get it occasionally," she said later. "I think it's because I was tired. … I'm pretty tired right now. My legs hurt." Tired as she was, her long legs and long drives held up on Saturday. Michelle beat the U.S. amateur champion, Becky Lucidi. Then she outclassed Aimee Cho to make the thirty-six-hole final on Sunday.

Winning Her First Title

Now all that stood between Wie and the title was Virada Nirapathpongporn. A native of Bangkok, Thailand, and a former U.S. college champion, she was eight years older than Michelle. She played tough,

FACT FILE

Virada Nirapathpongporn's college friends called her "Oui" for short. In French, *oui* means "yes" and sounds like WEE. So, in the Publinx final, it was … Oui versus Wie!

but Wie was too much for her. "Michelle played great," she conceded when the final round was over. "She was one shot better. That's why she deserved to win — why she's holding that big trophy."

Michelle's most memorable moment came on the twenty-fourth hole of the match. Her older opponent played it safe on the 479-yard (438-m) hole. She used three strokes to reach the green and made the hole in five strokes, for a par.

Michelle started the hole with a huge drive. The ball sailed almost 320 yards (293 m), but it went wide. It landed in the sand, 180 yards (165 m) from the cup. A water hazard blocked its path to the green.

Powerful tee shots are the strongest part of Michelle's game. Here, she shows her form at the 2005 John Deere Classic.

Wie faced a tough choice. She could make a safe shot and be sure of avoiding the water. Or, she could make a bold move and aim straight for the cup. "I'm going for it," she said. Her shot sailed over the water and landed on the edge of the green. Two putts later, she had a birdie — and control of the match.

"Golf is more fun if you take risks," she said later. The reward was her first national title — the first of many that golf experts are sure will come her way.

On October 5, 2005, after announcing her decision to turn pro, Michelle went out on the course to show photographers what she does best.

ISLAND GIRL

Michelle Sung Wie was born on October 11, 1989, in Honolulu, Hawaii. Her father's full name is Byung Wook Wie, but he likes to be called B.J. Her mother, Hyun Kyong Wie, usually goes by the name Bo. B.J. and Bo grew up in Korea. They moved to Hawaii in 1988, the same year they got married.

B.J. and Bo

B.J. came to the United States in 1983. For nine months of the year, he teaches about transportation at the University of Hawaii. The other three months, he travels with Michelle while she competes. On the golf course, he often serves as her caddie.

Bo arrived in the United States in 1987. She buys and sells property in Honolulu. Bo was the first member of the family to play

Michelle and Tiger

When Michelle was growing up, her father stuck pictures of golf star Tiger Woods on her bedroom wall. He wanted her to learn from Tiger's sweet swing. Today, as a young golf star, Wie is often compared to Woods.

In August 2005, Michelle appeared on David Letterman's late-night TV show. "Do you know Tiger Woods?" he asked her. She answered that she had met him once. "I was really dumbstruck," she admitted. "I was like zoned out. If he said anything to me, I didn't listen!"

A huge photo of Tiger looms over Michelle as she tees off at the seventh hole of the 2005 John Deere Classic.

golf. Back in Korea, she was a champion golfer, although she laughs about it now. When a reporter for *Golf World* magazine asked her about her title, Bo said she only had to beat four decent golfers to win it.

Crash Course

Bo taught B.J. how to play golf. Soon, they were golfing as a couple. Michelle joined in the fun, too. "I just loved driving the golf cart and, you know, being with them," she told David Letterman on his television show, *The Late Show with David Letterman*. "It was awesome. And that's how I started."

Michelle's parents got her a set of junior clubs when she was four. Within a year, she could drive the ball 100 yards (91 m). She began practicing on a baseball field. She told Letterman that by the time she was five or six, she could hit the ball

FACT FILE

Michelle has intelligence to match her talent and beauty. She says she knew most of her letters by her first birthday and could read by the time she turned two.

Bo's Health Tips

In a 2004 interview, Wie talked about a special health drink her mom gets for her at a Korean food store in Los Angeles. "They kill a goat and put it in a pressure cooker until the meat falls off," Michelle said. "Then they add some kind of snake, a little ginseng and some herbs. They strain the juice and put it in a pouch, and you're supposed to drink it. It's like vomit mixed with coffee, totally disgusting. But it really increases my strength and stamina. I complain, but as my mom points out, I drink the whole thing twice a day."

over the outfield fence. After she broke a couple of windows, she said, her parents began taking her to a driving range.

The family stopped golfing together when Michelle was nine years old. Her parents say the fees were getting too high. But Michelle has a different story. "They stopped playing because I'd gotten better than them," she told a reporter for *Golf World* magazine.

FACT FILE

Michelle played her first full eighteen-hole round of golf when she was seven. She finished at 14 over par. This score is better than the average for golfers of any age.

PHENOM

At the age of ten, Wie began working with golf coach Casey Nakama. Casey is one of Hawaii's top golfers. He teaches junior golfers at the Olomana Links. This course is near the Wie family home in Honolulu, on the island of Oahu.

Casey soon began singing the praises of his young student. "She's a phenom," he said to a local reporter, referring to Wie's phenomenal ability. "There's no high school girl in Hawaii who can hit the ball longer than her." Casey saw big promise in Wie. "Obviously she's big," he told an interviewer in 2001. "She had a lot of

FACT FILE

Michelle loves sports. She played baseball as a young girl. She also tried basketball, soccer, gymnastics, and tennis. She jokes that she chose golf over tennis because she doesn't like to run.

physical ability with her size for her age. You can always work with potential like that."

At Olomana, Michelle showed that the rest of her game was improving along with her driving. In 2000, while only in sixth grade, she shot a 64 on the full-size, 5,400-yard (4,938-m) course.

Playing to Win

Wie entered her first real tournament in 1999, an event run by the Oahu Junior Golf Association. Michelle competed in the "Girls 10 & Under" class. On a par-57 course, she shot a 31 on the front nine, taking a big lead. She lost the lead on the back nine and finished in a tie. But she sealed the victory in a playoff.

Soon, she was winning tournaments easily — too easily. To get better, she would have to play against better golfers.

FACT FILE

The National Golf Foundation reports that more than 27 million Americans play golf. Of these, almost 3 million are between twelve and seventeen years old.

Practice, Practice, Practice

When Michelle was in the eighth grade, she discussed her practice routine with *Golf for Women* magazine. During the school year, she practices about four hours a day. On weekends, her daily sessions last up to eight hours. First, she works on her driving by whacking five buckets of balls. Next, she spends three quarters of an hour on shorter shots. Lastly, she heads onto the course for the fun part — her daily round of golf.

Wie needs to improve her short game if she wants to beat the best. Here, she makes a chip shot at the 2005 U.S. Amateur Public Links Championship at Shaker Run Golf Club in Ohio.

Traveling to the Mainland

In July 2000, Michelle entered a major tournament on the mainland. For the ten-year-old and her parents, it was a huge step. The tournament took place in North Carolina, a long way from home. The airfare alone cost Michelle and her parents almost five thousand dollars. "It's expensive," she admitted. "But my parents and I think it's worth it."

This tournament was Wie's first Publinx. It was held at the 6,146-yard (5,620-m), par-72 Legacy Golf Links course. A total of 144 women entered.

Michelle's father, B.J. Wie, was her caddie when she competed at the Weetabix Women's British Open in 2005.

Each had qualified by winning a regional competition. Not only was Michelle the youngest person to qualify, she was also the youngest woman ever to play in the tournament.

Wie's score for the first thirty-six holes was 150, or six over par. She finished in the top twenty but lost her first playoff match. Michelle didn't putt well, and she didn't play her best game. But she didn't embarrass herself, either.

The next month, a call came from the *Tonight Show with Jay Leno*. Leno wanted her to come on the show as a guest. The offer was tempting, but B.J. said no. A time for television appearances would come later. Right now, B.J. thought, the Wie family had more important work to do. They had to get the nation's newest golf superstar ready for sixth grade.

FACT FILE

Each year, U.S. golfers spend more than $24 billion on golf equipment and course fees. They spend another $26 billion or more on golf-related travel.

CHAPTER 4

PLAYING AGAINST THE GUYS

Michelle Wie won't settle for being the best female golfer. She wants to be the best player, period — male or female. A family friend once told her she could be the next Se Ri Pak. The friend meant it as a compliment. After all, Se Ri Pak was the top Korean golfer on the women's pro tour. But Michelle frowned. She didn't want to be the next Se Ri Pak. She wanted to be the next Tiger Woods.

Working on Her Game

Golf coach Gary Gilchrist began working with Wie in 2002. He does nothing to

FACT FILE

Tiger Woods has doubts about Michelle's decision to compete against the world's best while she's still so young. She needs "to play and win" and "learn the art of winning," he says.

Making the Cut

A few of the greatest female golfers have tried to compete against men. Babe Didrikson was an outstanding golfer from the 1930s to the 1950s. She starred in just about every sport she tried. When asked if there was anything she didn't play, she said, "Yeah, dolls." At the 1932 Olympics in Los Angeles, she entered three events. She won gold medals and set world records in two of them — high hurdles and the javelin throw.

Didrikson took up golf seriously in the mid-1930s. In 1945, she became the first female golfer to "make the cut" (qualify) for the championship rounds of a major men's event. Her score after thirty-six holes was good enough to allow her to compete for the championship.

In May 2003, another great golfer, Annika Sorenstam, tried to compete against men. She entered the Colonial, a men's pro tour event. While thousands of people cheered, she shot a one-over-par 71 on the first day. On the second day, however, she ballooned to a 74. Her 145 for thirty-six holes missed the cut by four strokes. She was disappointed, but still upbeat. "I really tested myself," Sorenstam said. "That's why I'm here. I have a lot to be proud of." Se Ri Pak made the cut in a Korean men's event in October 2003.

Coach Gary Gilchrist caddied for Michelle at the 2003 U.S. Women's Open.

discourage her ambition. "She needs to mature, play with the best, learn from the best, and beat the best," he says.

"There's not a lot of young kids that can hit as far as she can," Gilchrist notes. But in order to be the best, he says, she needs to work on her all-around game. He calls the short game the weakest part of her play. "If she's going to be a champion, she needs to know how to play every shot in the bag."

Doing the "Unbelievable"

Michelle has been playing against men for a long time. The Manoa Cup is Hawaii's top men's amateur tournament. In 2001, when Wie was eleven, she became the first female and the youngest player to qualify. In 2002, she was also the first female to compete in Hawaii's Pearl Open. A year later, as a thirteen-year-old at the Pearl, she was the youngest ever to make the cut.

FACT FILE

The winner of the Sony Open in 2004 was Ernie Els. He played a practice round with Michelle before the tournament began. In 2003, Michelle said that she tried to pattern her swing after his.

Going Long

Tiger Woods is the best player in men's golf, and he is also near the top in terms of driving distance. On the 2005 pro tour, Tiger's tee shots averaged about 315 yards (288 m) — more than three times the length of a football field.

As a fifteen-year-old, Michelle's tee shots averaged at least 280 yards (256 m). From the tee, Wie is more than 10 yards (9 m) better than the top woman pro, Annika Sorenstam. But Michelle's average ranks her only about 150th among the men. With strength training, she hopes to add 15 to 20 yards (14 to 18 m) to her average drive.

All eyes were on Michelle when she played in the Sony Open in Hawaii in January 2004. Teeing off against some of the world's best male golfers, she shot a two-over-par 72 on the first eighteen holes. With her drives soaring more than 300 yards (274 m), she did even better on the next eighteen. She putted extremely well and birdied two of the last three holes for a 68. She missed the cut by just one stroke. Michelle beat 47 men in a field of 144. Of the men she tied or beat, 25 were previous winners on the men's pro tour.

The pros were amazed. "To do what she did was unbelievable," said golf legend Arnold Palmer. "She will change the game, without question, with her golfing. She's going to attract people that even Tiger didn't attract, young people, both boys and girls, and families."

For years, Michelle has been one of Hawaii's most famous people. Here, she speaks at the state capitol alongside Governor Linda Lingle.

FACT FILE

Paula Creamer is another teenage golf star. She and Michelle played for the U.S. team that won the 2004 Curtis Cup. This women's competition pits a U.S. team against a team of British and Irish players. In her first pro season in 2005, Paula earned more than $1 million.

HIGH HOPES, NEAR MISSES

Living up to your own image can be tough. In 2005, Michelle did amazing things for a girl of fifteen. But a lot of people have very high hopes for her, and anything less than a win can seem disappointing.

On the LPGA Tour

Although still an amateur, Michelle took part in several major Ladies Professional Golf Association (LPGA) tournaments in the summer of 2005. In June, she competed in

FACT FILE

If Michelle had been a pro golfer while competing in the Weetabix Women's British Open, she would have earned more than $120,000. But because she was an amateur and still in school, she was not allowed to accept the big paycheck.

Finding Balance

Michelle Wie is fortunate. She loves what she does. She loves her family. She teases her father, and he teases back. They appear to have a very strong relationship.

Not all young golf stars are so lucky. Consider the example of Beverly Klass. Like Michelle, she started playing golf at a very early age. Hitting golf balls is about all she can remember from her childhood. That, and her father's anger when she played badly. Her father made her turn pro when she was only ten years old.

"He did some good things and he did some bad things," Klass told a Florida newspaper in 2003. "Our family pretty much lived in misery. ... He'd never tell me how pretty I looked. Everything was always based on my performance. When I'd hit one bad shot, he'd be cussing me from the sidelines." Klass remembered one time when her father took a belt and beat her so hard she bled.

The Florida reporter asked Klass if she had some advice for the Wie family. "There are going to be some sort of sacrifices you have to make," Klass answered. "But I would say, let her go out with friends, go to the movies, the beach, church, whatever. Just try to be a kid and do what a kid does. You've got to have the balance. Otherwise, you become unbalanced."

Wie was the top amateur at the Weetabix Women's British Open in 2005. She also tied for third among all the competitors.

the McDonald's LPGA Championship in Maryland. Annika Sorenstam, the heavy favorite, shot an 11-under-par 277 to win. Wie came in second with 280, and she shot a 69 on the pressure-packed final eighteen holes. Among all the greats in women's golf, Michelle was the only player in the tournament to beat par in all four rounds.

Later that same month, she played in the U.S. Women's Open in Colorado. Playing against the world's best women golfers, she was tied for the lead after the first fifty-four holes. On the final eighteen, however, she shot bogey after bogey. Her one-day score was an 11-over-par 82. It was one of her worst days ever.

In late July, she traveled to England for the Weetabix Women's British Open. She was shaky at the start. Her score for the first eighteen holes was a wobbly 75. But her scores in the next three rounds sizzled: 67, 67, and 69. She finished tied for third place with a 10-under-par 278. On the final day, she even outplayed the great Annika, who shot 71 and tied for fifth.

Dollar Signs

Wie started eleventh grade in the autumn of 2005. On October 5, six days before her sixteenth birthday, she announced that she was turning pro. She said she planned to finish high school. She also said she would like to go to college. Turning pro allowed her to sign major deals with Nike and Sony. Other big contracts are likely to follow.

One golfer who thinks it's okay for Michelle to go pro at such an early age is men's champion Johnny Miller. "She's a one-in-a-hundred-million golfer," he says.

Michelle told David Letterman she thought turning pro wouldn't put too much pressure on her. "I love playing for money," she said. "We used to play like, always, like for five dollars a round. The only difference is I'm not going to be playing for five-dollar rounds anymore. It's going to be a lot bigger."

FACT FILE

Michelle's deals with Sony and Nike will pay her up to $10 million. On the day she turned pro, she said she would give $500,000 to help victims of Hurricane Katrina.

TIME LINE

1989   Michelle Sung Wie is born October 11, in Honolulu, Hawaii.

1994   Begins playing golf at the age of four.

1999   Wins her first junior tournament in Hawaii.

2000   At ten, competes in Publinx, a national women's event.

2001   Wins two women's tournaments.

2003   At thirteen, she becomes the youngest winner of the Publinx women's title.

2004   Competing against top men in Sony Open, comes within one shot of making cut. Helps U.S. win Curtis Cup against team from Britain and Ireland.

2005   Finishes second behind Annika Sorenstam at the McDonald's LPGA Championship in June. On October 5, she announces her decision to turn pro.

2006   In May, finishes first in local qualifier for men's U.S. Open. At sixteen, becomes youngest female to make cut in professional male tour event for the SK Telecom Open. *Time* magazine names her one of "100 People Who Shape Our World."

GLOSSARY

amateur — someone who competes in a sport without being paid.

back nine — the last nine holes on an eighteen-hole golf course.

birdie — a score of one stroke under par on a hole.

bogey — a score of one stroke over par on a hole. A double-bogey is two strokes over par.

caddie — during a golf match, a person who carries a player's clubs and helps in other ways.

front nine — the first nine holes on an eighteen-hole golf course.

green — on a golf course, the mostly level area of smooth, short grass at the end of a hole that surrounds the cup and flagstick.

par — the number of strokes a golfer is expected to need to finish a hole or the entire course.

Publinx — short for U.S. Women's Amateur Public Links Championship.

putter — a golf club used on the green.

stamina — the ability to keep going and stay strong.

tournament — a series of games or contests.

TO FIND OUT MORE

BOOKS

Michelle Wie: She's Got the Power! High Five Reading
   (series). Cynthia A. Dean (Edge Books)

The Young Golfer: A Young Enthusiast's Guide to Golf.
   Richard Simmons (DK Publishing)

VIDEOS

Golf: Links in Time (A&E Home Video) NR

Tiger: The Authorized DVD Collection (Buena Vista) NR

WEB SITES

808Golf.com: Michelle Wie
www.808golf.com/michellewie/default.htm
Photos, videos, and additional information about Michelle

LPGA.com
www.lpga.com
Official site of the Ladies Professional Golf Association

Seoul Sisters.com
www.seoulsisters.com
A good fan site devoted to Korean and Korean-American
   female golfers

INDEX

About the Author

Geoffrey M. Horn has been a fan of music, movies, and sports for as long as he can remember. He has written more than two dozen books for young people and adults, along with hundreds of articles for encyclopedias and other works. He lives in southwestern Virginia, in the foothills of the Blue Ridge Mountains, with his wife, their collie, and four cats. He dedicates this book to the memory of his father, his first (and last) golf teacher.